THE GREAT BOOK

CHEETAHS

FOR KIDS

To Dudas,

May all your dreams come true.

The great Book about Cheetahs ©2019
Text and illustrations by G. Guarita and Qwerty Books.
All rights reserved.
ISBN: 9798602887501

QWERTY
BOOKS

A WORD FROM THE AUTHOR

From cheetahs to lizards, from dolphins to dinosaurs, from space to how things work, all that and everything in between, fascinated me growing up.

In different ways, I was blessed with the priceless fortune of growing up in a house full of amazing books. I spent my childhood breathing stories in endless pages with amazing pictures, having fun and learning wonderful and incomparable lessons that I have carried with me throughout my life and passed on to my children and students.

Because I love to teach what I learn, I wrote The Great Book About Cheetahs, so you too can learn, feel and have fun the same way that I learned, felt and had fun growing up surrounded by fascinating books.

So buckle up! It's time to discover The Great Book About Cheetahs for Kids.

G. Guarita

Welcome to the amazing world of the cheetah, a fascinating creature, and the fastest land animal in our planet. Cheetahs are wonderful animals: caring parents, fantastic hunters, and with a body tailor-made for speed.

In this book you will learn all about what makes the cheetah such a beautiful and majestic symbol of power, elegance, and beauty: you will learn about their size, weight, and strength; about their hunting abilities and habits; about their habitat, different species and family members; and many more interesting facts, in this Great Book About Cheetahs.

Once, the swift cats rolled free wide across the African and Asian continents, but now they only inhabit about 10 percent of their historic range. They are confined mostly to dry open grasslands of Sub-Saharan Africa, and predominantly in parks and natural reserves.

Scientists estimate that the population of cheetahs in 1900 was of more than 100,000 animals. Sadly, today there are only around 9,000 to 12,000 cheetahs left in the world. This wonderful animal is now listed as an endangered species.

The cheetah is found mainly in the eastern and southern regions of Africa, but the range in eastern Africa has been reduced to a portion of its original extent. A few isolated populations occur in the Sahara, and in low numbers in northern and western Africa.

A small population of about 200 animals still exists in northeastern Iran, but it is highly endangered. There is also the possibility of existing cheetahs in Afghanistan and Turkmenistan, but this has not been confirmed.

HABITAT

Historic range

Confirmed
  populations
    in existence

Possible
  populations
    in existence

Hare

Wildebeest

Impala

Ostrich

Thompson's gazelle

Zebra

Warthog

A CHEETAH'S MEAL

Cheetahs are fantastic hunters, fast and watchful, and always on the lookout for the next meal. Like all cats, cheetahs are carnivores, meaning they only eat meat, which they obtained from the animals they hunt.

These big cats live of prey they hunt in the open prairies and vast grasslands. They usually go for the medium size animals that can be taken down by speed rather than by force.

Cheetahs usually prey on Grant's gazelle, impala, reedbuck, springbok, and Thomson's gazelle. But they also chase smaller prey like birds, foxes, hares and other small rodents.

When hunting in group, cheetahs can dare to hunt bigger prey, like the wildebeest, oryx, ostrich, warthog, and zebra.

Did you know ?

Cheetahs are perfectly adapted to their environment, the dry planes of Africa and Iran, where water is scarce. But that's not a problem for our great cat: a cheetah can survive with only one drink every three to four days, getting the rest of the fluids it needs from prey's meat and organs.

When hunting, the fast cat relies on its fantastic eyesight to spot prey, and in its spotted tawny coat to stay undetected and creep up as close as possible, to the right target.

And then, the cheetah deploys its "secret weapon": an astonishing ability to run at a top speed of over 100 km/h (62 mph), and to go from 0 to 80 km/h (50 mph) in just three seconds. Enough to catch even the most attentive of animals by surprise.

But as if that wasn't enough, cheetahs are not only fast, they are swift too, making use of their semi-retractable claws and muscular long tail to take very sharp turns at very high speeds.

All this allows cheetahs to catch up and knock down or make their victim trip, and fall. And it all ends up with a hasty bite to the throat.

After a successful hunt, cheetahs usually hide their kill, dragging it into tall grass. This prevents the meal from getting stolen by other predators or scavengers.

It's not easy for a cheetah to defend its food, and usually the fast cat avoids a fight all together, ignoring the attacker or running away instead.

Cheetahs have fragile bodies, build for speed rather than for strength, and even a little damage to their body can be very disastrous.

Fortunately, their high speed and acceleration allows the cats to escape any predator within no time.

Halfway between a lion's pride and the leopard's solitude, cheetahs can have different kinds of social interactions. In the wild, they can are found alone, but can also form groups, usually with 2 to 6 members, called coalitions.

Female cheetahs usually live and hunt alone, only getting together with males from time to time, to mate. They form temporary groups, consisting of a mother and its young. Mother cheetahs will stay from 16 to 18 months with their litters, until the young ones are ready to face the world on their own.

Solitary cheetahs tend to be semi-nomadic, living in home ranges that occupy areas as big as 829 square km (320 square mi.). They will rarely remain in an area for more than a few days, sometimes following herds of prey in their migrations.

Coalitions are territorial, and will defend their ground against other males, but rarely to the death. A coalition's territory can cover the home ranges of several females.

DID YOU KNOW?

Scientists define "**home range**" as the area in which an animal lives and moves on a periodic basis. Unlike a **territory**, which the animal will actively defend, home ranges are unguarded, and can often overlap each other.

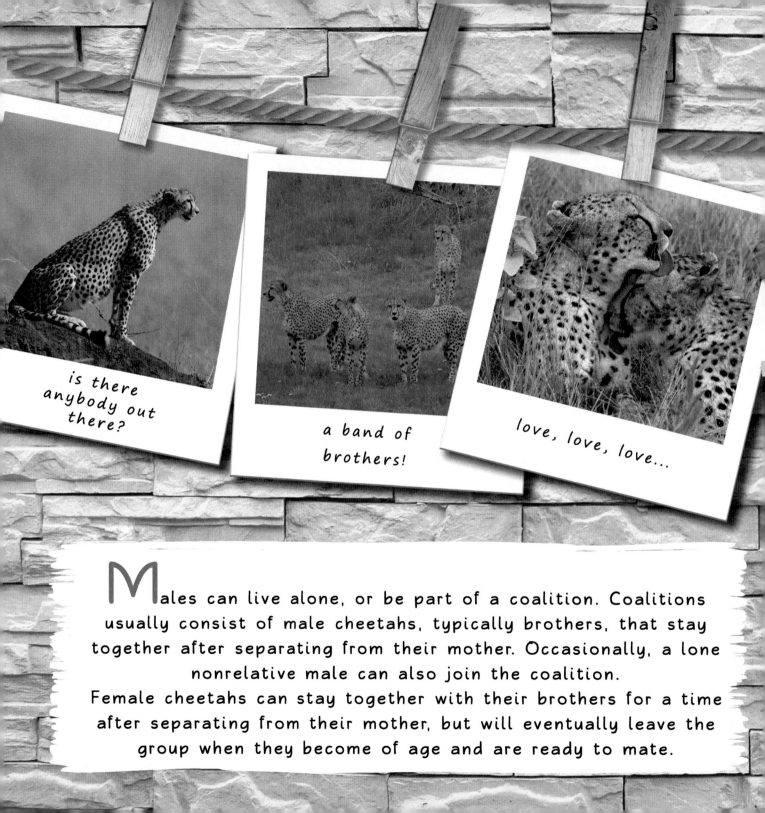

is there anybody out there?

a band of brothers!

love, love, love...

Males can live alone, or be part of a coalition. Coalitions usually consist of male cheetahs, typically brothers, that stay together after separating from their mother. Occasionally, a lone nonrelative male can also join the coalition.

Female cheetahs can stay together with their brothers for a time after separating from their mother, but will eventually leave the group when they become of age and are ready to mate.

"I'm going for a
walk in the park!"

"do any of you spot
our dinner?"

nap time...

Cheetahs in a coalition will live and hunt together, often for the rest of their lives. Members spend much time together, and form a very close bound. They spend time grooming and cleaning each other, and if any member becomes separated or lost, the rest of the group will look and call out for him.

Although male cheetahs don't participate in raising their young, female cheetahs are caring, affectionate and dedicated mothers. A mommy cheetah usually gives birth to between two and eight cubs at a time, usually in a secluded lair well hidden by tall vegetation.

Baby cheetahs are born weighing somewhere from 150 grams to 300 grams, blind and helpless. They are often the target of other predators, so in the first five to six weeks the mother will stay with the young as much as possible, leaving them only to hunt.

MOMMIES AND CUBS

With around six weeks, cheetah cubs are now very active and curious, but also very eager to learn. They start following their mom on her hunting rounds, accompanying her at a close distance, learning all the essential skills they will need to survive in the wild.

Did you know?

When raising her cubs, mother cheetahs will often change lairs, every four days or so. The new lair is generally only within a few meters of the older one, but this is enough to prevent the buildup of smells, which can attract predators like hyenas.

Now with 6 months of age, the young cheetahs stop drinking mom's milk, and only eat meat. Mom still does most of the hunting, but the cubs are encouraged to join the action. The mother will frequently catch the prey alive, releasing it in front of the cubs. The young cats will then chase the semi-stunned victim and try to strike it down, always under mom's watchful eye.

Cubs typically stay with their mothers for 16 to 18 months. By then the younglings are ready to face the world on their own. Usually the young males will continue living together, often for life, while the females will leave the group, to find a mate and raise their own families.

The long and slim body puncturing the air... The tall slander legs barely touching the ground... The large thick tail leaping from side to side... It is something unforgettable, the ight of a cheetah running at full speed in the wild.

The cheetah's slender body is covered with a tawny, pale buff or grayish-white fur coat, dotted with black spots. This tan and shaded pattern lets the cheetah blend easily with the tall grasses of the savannahs, allowing the cat to get is near as possible to its pray.

Cheetahs can have somewhere between 2,000 and 3,000 spots. The black fur actually grows out of the black spots on their skin, and forms a unique pattern to each cat. Much like our own fingerprints, these patterns are used by scientist and locals to individually identify each cheetah.

THE CHEETAH'S BODY

Cheetahs usually grow to between 1,1 and 1,5 meters (3.6 to 4.9 feet), and weigh from 21 kg to 72 kg (46 to 159 pounds). Their powerful tails usually measure between 65 cm to 80 cm (2 to 2.6 feet). Male cheetahs are usually heavier and larger than females.

Like our own house cats, cheetahs can't roar. They can purr, and make around 14 different sounds. Often, cheetahs make chirping-like sounds, when communicating with each other. By the way, the only cats that can roar are lions, tigers, leopards and jaguars.

BORN TO RUN

Most of the cat species, from tigers, to leopards, to our house cats, hunt by stalking and ambushing their preys. They then make use of their strong legs and sharp claws, to jump on target and bring it down. But cheetahs are different. Speed, not power, is the cheetah's weapon of choice.

Cheetahs are truly built for speed. A cheetah's entire body is adapted for a single purpose — run as fast as possible, as quickly as possible. For this, cheetahs rely on a long and slender body, tall legs, and a spring like, flexible spine.

To control all that speed, the cheetah possesses a long muscular tail, and highly adapted paws and claws. They allow the cat to make very sharp turns at high speeds, always keeping up with its prey.

Did you know ?

Even at full speed, cheetahs are able to maintain their heads very still, barely moving them while sprinting. This helps them to hold an incredibly still gaze on their prey while in hot pursuit.

Cheetahs use their long muscular tails as rudders, swinging them from side to side, when making a curve. This helps them to always keep their balance, even in the sharpest turns.

Being the world's land speed champion means the cheetah's body requires a lot of oxygen to push those muscles, when running at full speed. So, cheetahs have an enlarged heart, capable of pumping oxygen rich blood to their whole body at a very high rate. They also have large nostrils, capable of taking all that oxygen in. And that really come in handy, because the breathing rate of a cheetah goes from 60 to 150 breaths a minute, while running.

Cheetahs have an especially flexible spine, that works like a spring, when running. This gives the cat an extra impulse at each stride (the length between steps), making it as long as a galloping horse's stride – 6 to 7 meters (21 feet). Their feet only touch the ground twice during each stride.

Unlike other cats, cheetahs don't retract their claws completely. The claws' main purpose is to grip the floor as much as possible during the acceleration and the run, and not to strike prey. Their paws are also harder than other cats, allowing them a better grip while sprinting.

Usually, a predator relies on one or two enhanced senses to hunt. But cheetahs are gifted cats: not only do these fantastic animals have a great eyesight, but they also have a very sensible nose, and are able to hear the slightest sound over a great distance.

To locate its preys over a distance, the cheetah relies first of all on its sensitive nose. Scientists believe that this big cat is able to identify and follow herds of its favorite prey from a far, by smelling them from over 5 km (3 miles) away.

We, humans, can see clearly what is in front of us, within a fairly narrow viewpoint. But we are no match for the cheetah, as this cat can see across a much wider field of vision - 210 degrees versus ours 140. Cheetahs can spot their prey anywhere within all of its surroundings, allowing them to pick the right target, but also to keep the target in sight while pursuing it.

SENSES

Cheetahs have excellent hearing, so incredibly strong they can easily hear any sound from over a 5 mile (8 km) radius.

And if all of that wasn't impressive enough, there is more: recent studies on the cheetah's inner ear suggest that it is highly specialized, evolved to help the cat detect even the slightest bobbing or tilting of the cheetah's head. This helps the cat to keep its head very balanced and still during a full speed chase, always keeping its eyes on the prize.

LEOPARD

DOMESTIC CAT

IBERIAN LYNX

CARACAL

The cheetah (Acinonyx jubatus) is a large cat, and the fastest among the Felidae family. This family also includes tigers, lions, caracals, lynxes, and our domestic cats, among others.

Cheetah fossils found in Tanzania date back to about three million years, suggesting that these amazing cats have been running on earth since then.

BOBCAT

TIGER

LION

CHEETAH

THE CHEETAH'S FAMILY

CHEETAH CUBS

Cheetahs are classified in the genus Puma, along with the cougar and the jaguarundi.

Although the cheetah is an Old World cat, some evidence indicates that the three species of the Puma lineage possibly had a common ancestor in North America, around 8 million years ago.

COUGAR

CHEETAHS

JAGUARUNDI

owadays the IUCN's Cat Classification Task Force recognizes four different cheetah subspecies:

<u>Acinonyx Jubatus Soemmeringii</u> – The Northeast African cheetah is native to South Sudan, Ethiopia and Eritrea. Physically, this subspecies resembles the Southeast African cheetah, to which it is closely related. Fairly large, the Northeast African cheetah it is the darkest in fur colour, with distinctive white patches around its eyes. This subspecies tail is also notably thick.

Did you know?

IUCN stands for International Union for Conservation of Nature. It is the global authority on the status of the natural world and the measures needed to safeguard it.

CHEETAH SUBSPECIES

<u>Acinonyx Jubatus Jubatus</u> – The Southeast African cheetah is the most numerous of all the cheetahs subspecies. It is native to East and Southern Africa, and lives mainly in the lowlands and deserts of the Kalahari, the savannahs of Okavango Delta, the farmlands in Namibia, and the grasslands in South Africa. This cheetah has usually a bright yellow or golden coat, with a very distinctive white underside. Its fur is slightly thicker than that of other subspecies.

Acinonyx Jubatus Hecki – The Northwest African cheetah, also known as the Saharan cheetah, is native to the Sahara Desert and the Sahel. It differs in appearance from other African cheetahs, being somewhat smaller in size, and with a shorter coat, which can be nearly white in colour. Its spots fade from black to light brown, and the tear stripes are often missing. Listed as Critically Endangered, it is estimated that there are less than 250 Northwest African cheetahs left in the wild.

<u>Acinonyx</u>
<u>Jubatus</u>
<u>Venaticus</u> –
Classified as
Critically
Endangered, the
Asiatic cheetah is
confined to Iran, the
only surviving
population in Asia. It
used to occur from the
Arabian Peninsula to India. The Asiatic
cheetah's fur colour ranges from buff to
fawn, with black stripes on the tail tip,
and a shorter coat and mane than
African cheetahs.

Cheetahs are wild animals, great hunters and with a strong self-preservation instinct. But they are also caring parents, compassionate brothers and, being shy and cautious animals, pose no direct threat to humans.

Byzantine bowl with cheetah

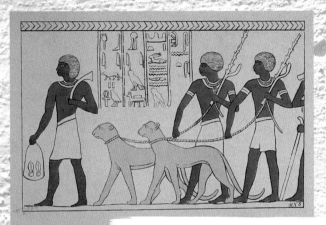
A hieroglyph depicting leashed cheetahs. Deir el-Bahari, Luxor, Egypt.

Since old times, cheetahs have enchanted us, with their calm temperament, physical attributes and stunning beauty. Dating back to 3000 B.C., Sumerians would train cheetahs for hunting, and in old Egypt, cheetahs were common pet animals for the royalty, sometimes lavishly adorned with collars and leashes.

In the middle east, Cheetahs would accompany the nobility to hunts, sometimes in special seats behind saddles. And the Indian Mughal ruler Akbar the Great (1556-1605) is said to have kept as many as 1000 cheetahs.

Attendants of the Nawab of Oudh, with hunting cheetahs. Oudh State, India

CHEETAHS & US

Cheetahs are truly fascinating animals. But, unfortunately, nowadays cheetahs are under great threat of survival, due to its drastic population decline. Habitat loss is one of their biggest threats, as cheetahs seem to require a large area to live in. Also they can fall victim of hunters, or of farmers who attempt to protect their cattle, even though our wonderful cat is not known to prey on livestock.

Each cheetah is unique and irreplaceable, one of the most stunning creatures of our planet. No wild cat is more beautiful, no land animal is faster... What a shame, if we were not able to protect and keep for future generations the right to see, to admire and to love this marvelous animal for themselves!

Photo Credits

Cover - Pixabay Front Page - Derek Keats/Flickr Intro - Nigel
Swales/Pixabay Index - jjmusgrove/Flickr
A Cheetah's Meal - Bernard Dupont/Flickr; Paul Mannix/Flickr; Hein
Waschefort/Wikimedia; Charles J Sharp/Wikipedia; Lip kee
Yap/Flickr; JanMcCarthy/Pixabay; Ian Lindsay/Pixabay; Andrea
Bohl/Pixabay; Franziska/Pixabay
Hunting - Demetrius John Kessy/Flickr; Michel Espig/Flickr; Dr
Zoltan/Pixabay; Megan Coughlin/Flickr
Hunting (2nd Page) - nadine87/Pixabay; Åsa Berndtsson/Flickr;
Joris Leermakers/Flickr; Roel Roelofs/Pixabay; ChrisFiedler/Pixabay
Cheetahs and Cheetahs - Stuart Price/Kenya Photo
Cheetahs and Cheetahs (2nd Page) - Stuart Price/Kenya Photo;
Andrew Seaman/Flickr; Arturo de Frias Marques/Wikimedia;
GGuarita; Genevieve Desilets/Pixabay; Stuart Price/Kenya Photo
Mommies And Cubs - Siddharth Maheshwari/Wikimedia
Mommies And Cubs (2nd Page) - Greg Willis/Wikimedia; Daniel
Hahner/Pixabay; thdeprince/Pixabay
The Cheetah's Body - Derek Keats/Flikr; Roel Roelofs/Pixabay;
Sophia Hilmar/Pixabay; saltonnz/Pixabay
The Cheetah's Body (2nd Page) - Volker Glatsch/Pixabay
Born to Run - Susan Koppel/Animal Ark
Born to Run (2nd Page) - Gguarita
Senses - Demetrius John Kessy/Flickr
Senses (2nd Page) - Bernard Dupont/Flickr; Marty-arts/Pixabay
The Cheetah's Family - Programa Ex-Situ Conservação Do Lince
Ibérico; Gerhard Bogner/Pixabay; Leo Za1/Wikimedia; Robert
Greene/Pixabay; Skeeze/Pixabay; TeeFarm/Pixabay; Michael
Siebert/Pixabay; Martin Winkler/Pixabay; Eric Kilby/Flickr;
trebleclefmusic/Pixabay; Agencia Brasilia/Flickr
Cheetah Subspecies - Steve Wilson/Wikimedia; Joe
Zuccaro/Wikimedia; William Warby/Flickr; Wegmann/Wikimedia;
James Temple/Wikimedia; Arturo de Frias Marques/Wikimedia
Cheetah Subspecies (2nd Page) - Ehsan Kamali/Wikimedia; Erfan
Kouchari/Wikimedia; Christina Rogers/Flickr; Steve
Wilson/Wikimedia; Florence Devouard/Wikimedia
Cheetahs and Us - Metropolitan Museum of Art; Fæ/Wikipedia;
Emily Eden/British Library; nickyduplessis28/Pixabay

ISBN: 9798602887501

QWERTY BOOKS

Made in the USA
Las Vegas, NV
26 April 2021